POST-LIFE
INSTRUCTIONS
WORKBOOK

Leave directions for your body, funeral, reception, remembrance, affairs and more

VIDA FINIS™

Printed in the United States of America.

ISBN: 0-99-630502-5
ISBN: 978-0-99-630502-0

Design by Alan Barnett
Megaphone by Nico Ilk from the Noun Project

CONTENTS

1 Introduction

The event of our passing may truly be our final opportunity to be heard and impact others. At the time of our passing, our family and friends should follow any instructions we have provided and come together to honor our life.

So why is it that so many otherwise capable people fail to leave any meaningful instructions whatsoever for this most important event?

Do these people realize that they are not only losing their say as to *how they are treated, honored, and remembered* but that they are also missing the opportunity to *impact the experience of their loved ones?* Worse yet, by failing to provide clear directions on the most personal of topics they are increasing the decision-making burden of family and friends left behind.

Besides, if we don't leave instructions, then aren't we really saying some version of the following:

"Please allow a funeral home representative to make the key decisions as to what should happen to me."

"Please write a boilerplate obituary for me with the typical clichés."

"Select from the funeral home's list of over-priced options for my generic visitation and funeral."

"I don't want to impact how loved ones feel after I am gone or how they remember me."

"It is fine if my family and friends are stressed as they guess at my final wishes and try to sort out my affairs."

You don't need to be one of these people! Say NO to passive and generic and instead personalize the experience!

The *Post-Life Instructions Workbook* makes it *easy* (even enjoyable) to provide directions on the events marking your life and the experience you want for your loved ones.

This workbook captures all of the key questions in one place and provides *hundreds of suggestions,* in order to make it simple for you to:

- Specify how you want your body treated;

- Be described in the manner of your choosing;

- Design a visitation and/or funeral that suits you;

1

- Provide your loved ones with the experience you want for them;

- Make known how you want to be remembered;

- Provide administrative details and any other unique instructions; and

- Use your creativity to throw the end-of-life event of a lifetime!

How you use the *Post-Life Instructions Workbook* is up to you. It can be completed in twenty minutes or over several months. It can be updated frequently or never. You can complete the whole workbook or skip any chapters of your choosing.

You might provide very simple instructions such as, "Keep costs low no matter what," "Do not host the reception at a funeral home," or "Watch my favorite movie as a family every year." Or, you might choose to provide granular details from the venue, to the music or readings, the sequence of events, and the food. No matter what your instructions say, this workbook will ensure that your wishes are known. And each instruction you provide will be one less issue for your loved ones to need to resolve on their own.

The *Post-Life Instructions Workbook* is intended to cover all of the key topics and information that is relevant upon your passing (other than those legal items intended to be covered in a will).

Once you have completed this workbook, see chapter 9, where we have provided an easy, one-page summary to the extent you would like to make your instructions easier to share, including on Instagram, Facebook, or Twitter (#postlifeinstructions).

If desired, chapter 11 allows you to provide information on your personal affairs to make it easy for loved ones to have all the relevant details in one place. Additionally, chapter 12 includes blank pages to enable you to provide more detailed instructions than permitted by the spaces provided—or to address any unique topics or thoughts that are not otherwise covered in this workbook.

This workbook was designed to make post-life planning easy. By empowering you to make these decisions, this workbook can impact your attitude on the topics covered and can even be a fun group activity.

So why miss this opportunity? Let the *Post-Life Instructions Workbook* help you create and communicate your plan and desires. Don't make someone else decide for you. Your family and friends will greatly appreciate it—even if the funeral home representatives may not!

Tell your family and friends that you have completed the *Post-Life Instructions Workbook* and encourage them to complete one of their own!

2 Instructions

The *Post-Life Instructions Workbook* is designed to be a tool to help you easily convey your wishes on post-life topics. It is completely up to you how you use this workbook, but here are some suggestions:

1. Complete only those questions that are of interest to you. Feel free to be as brief or as detailed in your responses as you would like.

2. Use the blank pages in chapter 12 to provide a more detailed answer on any question than the space permits. Label your extended response using the question number so that it is easy to cross-refer.

3. If you would like, briefly summarize your responses using the summary in chapter 9 to make your desires easier to share. Post online using the hashtag #postlifeinstructions.

4. Sign and date the *Post-Life Instructions Workbook* in chapter 10. Make sure your family and friends know you have completed this workbook and where it can be found.

5. If you would like, complete chapter 11 to make it easy for loved ones to find relevant information regarding your personal affairs.

3 Obituary and Notifications

Describe me this way. No bad clichés.
And make sure the right people know.

For additional space on any response, use the blank pages in chapter 12 and cross-refer to the relevant question number.

3.A.   Do you want an obituary? (If no, please skip to question 3.J. below.)

   ☐ Yes   ☐ No

3.B.   If yes, do you want to include a brief biography or only name and birth and death dates?

_____

_____

_____

3.C.   Do you want a picture included with your obituary?

   ☐ Yes   ☐ No

3.D.   If yes, describe the type of picture you would like to use (e.g., what age, specify activity in picture, etc.), identify a specific picture or confirm you have included the picture with this workbook.

_____

_____

_____

3.E.   If you want an obituary, where would you like it published?

_____

_____

_____

Suggestions and examples			
Local / national paper, magazine, newsletter, billboard, etc.	Mailed / emailed to family, friends, coworkers, etc.	Posted in my favorite coffee shop, restaurant, bar, etc.	Turned into a painting or work of art
Posted to Facebook, Instagram, Twitter, other website / blog, etc. (if on my accounts, provide passwords)	Read aloud, posted, or distributed in my place of worship, military, fraternal, or service organization	Read in a public place (by person dressed as _____)	Name, birth, and death dates written in paint, chalk, etc. in a public place
Turned into audio or video recording and distributed or posted online	Posted on my door or in front of my house, apartment, living center, etc.	Sung by rock, pop, opera, gospel, R&B, blues, or rap artist	Skywriting name, birth, and death dates
Buried in time capsule			

3.F.   Have you written your own obituary?

☐ Yes   ☐ No

If yes, describe where it can be found or confirm you have included a copy with this workbook.

_____

_____

3.G. If not already written, what would you like your obituary to highlight?

_____

_____

_____

_____

_____

_____

_____

_____

Suggestions and examples			
Family (if desired, identify specific persons)	Faith, religious beliefs, or afterlife	Military service	Specific anecdote about me
Friends or others (if desired, identify specific persons)	Personal character	Religious, community, charitable or fraternal involvement	Hobbies, sports affiliations, interests, politics, etc.
Pet(s)	Sense of humor	Personal or professional accomplishments	My love of: _____
Birthday and/or birthplace	Specific words to describe my nature: _____	Vocation or employer	Specific period in my life
Age at death and/or cause of death	Education or intelligence	Travels	My home or my hosting of gatherings
Include invitation to visitation, funeral, or other events	My nickname	Physical attributes	

3.H.   If not already written, what do you NOT want your obituary to reference?

_____

_____

_____

_____

_____

_____

_____

_____

_____

_____

Suggestions and examples			
Age and/or birth date	Vocation or employer	Specific time in my life or anecdotes	Sadness, loss, etc.
Cause of death, health, or disability	Don't describe me as: _____	My politics or affiliation with: _____	Bad habits
Former spouse or other specific individuals	Physical attributes or appearance	Interests, hobbies, sports teams, etc.	My life before I was a person of faith
Don't list my family for privacy reasons	Religious beliefs	My background or education	Retirement home or living center
Don't include public invitation to visitation, funeral, or other events	God, afterlife, etc.	Time in the military	Income, wealth, or financial circumstances

3.I.   Do you have any other specific instructions for your obituary?

_____

_____

_____

_____

_____

Suggestions and examples			
Who should write it (family member, friend, professional, etc.)	Tone (e.g., upbeat, sorrowful, serious, intense, funny, etc.)	Describe how to honor or remember me	Funny photo (e.g., wrong person, stick figure, animal, photoshopped, etc.)
Use specific phrase, exclamation, or expletive	Theme (e.g., biographical, family, faith, career, travel, adventure, partly fictionalized, etc.)	Encourage service or gifts to charity (e.g., in lieu of flowers)	Special printing instructions (e.g., theme or colors, size and type of paper, etc.)
No use of clichés!	Include specific advice or quote: _____	Artwork accompanying obituary	Specific tagline: _____

3.J.   Do you have specific instructions regarding notifying others of your passing? If you would like to create a notification list, please use the blank pages in chapter 12 and cross-refer to the list below.

_____

_____

_____

_____

_____

4 Body

Here are my wishes. My loved ones need not trouble themselves with these decisions.

For additional space on any response, use the blank pages in chapter 12 and cross-refer to the relevant question number.

4.A.   What would you like to happen to your body upon your passing?

_____

_____

Suggestions and examples			
Buried	Cremated and ashes buried	Buried at sea	Mummification
Cremated	Eco-friendly burial (e.g., buried without embalming)	"Viking funeral," by burning body on pyre or boat	Turned into a mannequin
Buried or cremated within specified number of days	Eco-friendly cremation	Exposure or "sky funeral"	Dissolved in acid
Embalmed for viewing, visitation, and/or funeral, then cremated	Donate body or all or specified organs	Cryogenic freezing	Human composting
Perform autopsy before disposal of body	Partially buried (e.g., heart buried) and partially cremated		

4.B. If buried, what specific instructions do you have for your body?

_____

_____

_____

_____

Suggestions and examples			
What clothing / shoes or specific colors or materials	Particular hairstyle or hair color	Use my regular hairstylist or hire professional beautician	Wearing a mask, costume, face painting, crown, or tiara
Burial shroud	Particular look (e.g., "going out," beachwear, sleepwear, specific makeup, glasses, sunglasses, etc.)	Body positioning (e.g., alignment of arms, legs, and fingers, etc.)	Stake through my heart; coin or other item in mouth
Specific jewelry (e.g., wedding ring, earrings, necklace, cross, etc.)	Perfume or cologne	Write on my body or forehead	Humorous (e.g., middle finger up, pants down, etc.)

4.C. If body or ashes buried, what other specific instructions do you have? (See the following question 4.D. regarding marker or monument.)

_____

_____

_____

_____

Continued on next page

Body

_____

_____

_____

Suggestions and examples			
Casket details (e.g., type of wood, metal, or other material, color, lining, trim, oversized, full/half couch, etc.)	Timing of burial (e.g., prior to memorial service)	Entomb in mausoleum, mini-mausoleum, etc.	Bury me with religious text or other books, magazines, pictures, etc.
Decorate casket exterior or interior (e.g., initials or names, crest, team emblem, leopard print, unique shape)	Desired site for burial or entombment (e.g., specified cemetery, city or foreign country)	"Green" or natural burial (e.g., directly into dirt)	Bury me with cigarettes, alcohol, marijuana, candy, deck of cards, gun, etc.
Bury body in something other than casket	Same cemetery / vault as spouse, family, friend, pet, love interest, famous person, etc.	Conservation burial, where the fees fund the acquisition of land	Bury with my favorite: _____
Cardboard casket, mushroom suit, or other biodegradable encasement	Preferences for grave location (e.g., far from road, non flood zone, etc.)	Bury aligned with specific direction or geographical point	Hidden compartment in casket
I have already purchased casket and/or site of burial or entombment (provide details)	No public access to site or hidden grave (including map)	Flag or other item draped over casket	Instructions regarding burial vault, grave liner, lawn crypt, etc.
Do not purchase casket from funeral home	Be cheap or DON'T be cheap (or maximum / minimum cost)		

4.D. If buried, what instructions do you have for your marker or monument?

_____

_____

_____

_____

_____

_____

Suggestions and examples

Form of marker or monument (e.g., headstone, nameplate, footstone, slab, pillar, statue, cross, companion marker, or no marker)	Border or boundary around grave (by itself or together with other marker)	Preferred epitaph information for marker (e.g., specific name, whether to use birth and death dates, wife/mother, husband/father, veteran status, etc.)	Government furnished military marker or medallion
Type of material (e.g., granite, marble, bronze fieldstone, limestone, slate, quartzite, etc.).	Particular item used as marker (e.g., helmet, sword, bench, pile of stones, etc.)	Other epitaph message for marker (e.g., religious verse, Latin phrase, poem, funny saying, etc.)	Artwork, symbols, pictures, or other carving on marker
Shape, size, color, and finish of marker	Anonymous grave or dedicate marker after some period of time (e.g., in unveiling)	Style, font, and language for epitaph	Include accessories (e.g., vases, candle boxes, lamps, lights, etc.)
I have already purchased marker / monument (provide details)	Be cheap or DON'T be cheap (or maximum / minimum cost)	Hidden message, math problem, joke, etc. on marker	

4.E.　If cremated, what should happen to your ashes?

_____

_____

_____

_____

_____

Suggestions and examples			
Maintain with family or friends (and who specifically)	Spread where and by whom	Bury ashes and where (e.g., cemetery, backyard, memorial garden)	Mix with paint and make art or tattoo
What kind of receptacle (e.g., one or multiple, purchased urn, coffee can, cereal box, bottle, chest, etc.)	Spread in ancient place or other location having sentimental value	Entomb where (e.g., cremation niche or columbarium)	Use ashes to create memorial coral reef, hourglass, jewelry, phone case, sex toy, hood ornament, amulet, etc.
If urn, what features or design (e.g., biodegradable, shape, color, size, religious, engraving, printing or other decoration, etc.)	Scatter in the air, float ashes down a river, send out to sea, bury in time capsule, drop in volcano	Added to lawn, dirt, or fertilizer for impacting grass, garden, new tree, or plant	Use to fill stuffed animal, doll, or pillow
If urn, what material(s) (e.g., ceramic, wood, metal, stone, etc.)	Take ashes on a trip, limo ride, or mail to my favorite place or places I wanted to visit	Commingle with another person's ashes or other substance	Shoot out of gun, explode in fireworks, eat, snort, flush down toilet, put in car ashtray
I have already purchased urn (provide details)	Be cheap or DON'T be cheap (or maximum / minimum cost)	Do not purchase urn from funeral home	"Space burial" by launching ashes into outer space

5 Visitation or Reception

Generic is NOT ok. These are my instructions for a meaningful event.

For additional space on any response, use the blank pages in chapter 12 and cross-refer to the relevant question number.

5.A.   Would you like a visitation or reception for family and friends? (If no, please skip to chapter 6 of the *Post-Life Instructions Workbook*)

  ☐   Yes   ☐   No

5.B.   Would you like the event to take place before or in lieu of the funeral/memorial service? (Note that chapter 6 discusses preferences for events following the funeral/memorial service.)

  ☐   Before   ☐   In lieu of

5.C.   When would you like the event held (e.g., what time of day, when in relation to passing, etc.)?

_____

_____

_____

_____

5.D.   Should the event be open to the public or a private event?

  ☐   Public   ☐   Private

5.E.   Do you have a specific guest list?

☐ Yes   ☐ No

5.F.   If yes, specify whether the list is included with this workbook (e.g., using the pages in chapter 12) or where it can be found.

_____

_____

_____

_____

_____

5.G.   Who do you NOT want to attend the event? (Use the blank pages in chapter 12 for additional space.)

_____

_____

_____

_____

_____

5.H.   Do you want your body or ashes at the event?

☐ Yes   ☐ No

5.I.   If applicable, do you want an open or closed casket?

[ ] Open   [ ] Closed

5.J.   Where would you like the visitation or reception held?

_____

_____

_____

_____

_____

_____

_____

Suggestions and examples			
My home or someone else's	Reception hall or event venue	"Destination Memorial" away from home (e.g., favorite travel destination)	Bowling alley, batting cages, arcade, amusement park, or go-cart track
Graveside only ceremony at: _____	Restaurant, coffee shop, bar, or nightclub	Farm, ranch, or barn	Golf club or course, driving range, mini golf
Place of worship	Hotel	Park, woods, or around a campfire	Sports facility or field
Funeral home (or DON'T host at funeral home)	Museum, planetarium, or observatory	Beach, lake, or pool	Distillery, brewery, or vineyard
Military, fraternal, or service organization	Theatre	Public square or train station	Group field trip to: _____
My favorite place	Community center	Boat or party barge	

5.K.   What would you prefer the theme or mood of the visitation or reception to be like?

_____

_____

_____

_____

_____

_____

_____

_____

_____

_____

Suggestions and examples			
Traditional	Party, celebration of life, upbeat, etc.	Cocktail party	Mystery theme
Spiritual, religious, or afterlife	Sadness or loss	Sit down dinner or cookout	Costumes or dress up
Reflection of my life	Formal	Themed after my favorite things (e.g., hobbies, games, foods, sports teams, etc.)	Specific movie or TV show theme
Military or service theme	Unstructured and low key	Cards or game playing	Specific musical act or theme song
Funny	Irish wake	Sports, fishing, or hunting	Aliens or outer space

5.L. Do you want food, drink, and other offerings served at the event? If so, what?

_____

_____

_____

_____

_____

_____

_____

_____

_____

Suggestions and examples:			
Coffee and tea	My favorite dishes or type of food	Beer, wine, champagne, cocktails, open bar	Vegetarian or vegan food
Cake, cookies, candy	My famous recipe(s) for: _____	My favorite drink or a signature drink	Pizza or fried chicken
Nuts and party snacks	Catered from: _____	Marijuana or CBD edibles	McDonalds, Burger King, Taco Bell, Popeye's, etc.
Specific cake or cake with unique design (e.g., my picture, funny saying, etc.)	Ice cream truck, food truck, or hot dog stand	Cigarettes, cigars, e-cigarettes	Potluck style
Coffin-shaped or "R.I.P." cookies	Popcorn bar, candy bar, seafood bar, etc.		

5.M.   What features would you like for your visitation or reception? (Use the blank pages in chapter 12 for additional space.)

_____

_____

_____

_____

_____

_____

_____

_____

_____

_____

Suggestions and examples

Formal service (and who should officiate or be involved)	Procession line with my family	Guests bring a picture or a story to create a storyboard or storybook	Dress code or theme (e.g., formal, casual, specific colors, beachwear, costumes, etc.)
What is the most important feature (e.g., mood, food, decor, entertainment, etc.)	Open mic and/ or moderator who facilitates sharing memories about me	Create remembrance slideshow or video of my life or play one that I created	Guests wear nametags, including nature of relationship with me
Hire professional event planner	Specific verses, passages, poems, or literature to be read	Have guest book or other item to be signed and what should be done with it after (e.g., post comments online)	Use the reception to raise awareness or money for a cause

Continued on next page

How long should event last	Group prayer, singing, chanting, dancing	Hire a band or other musicians (e.g., cover band, mariachi band, harpist, violinist, bagpiper, etc.)	Outdoor activity (e.g., sports, bocce ball, croquet, bike ride, ice skating, hiking, picnic, scavenger hunt, etc.)
Arrange for transportation for: _____	Person of faith or bereavement counselor available to speak with guests	Play my favorite movie, TV show, album, playlist or song	Webcast or recorded by photographer or videographer
Be cheap or DON'T be cheap (or maximum / minimum cost)	If body present, specific instructions (e.g., viewing period)	Play games (e.g., cards, board games, trivia, charades, darts, pool or beer pong, etc.)	Body out of casket and posed (e.g., standing, playing cards, holding a drink, etc.)

5.N.   What decorations would you like to have at your visitation or reception?

_____

_____

_____

Suggestions and examples			
Pictures of me with family and friends	My art or other creative works	Cards or signs with details about my life or anecdotes	Specific flowers or floral design
Religious items	My favorite things (e.g., my collectibles, books, movies, tools, etc.)	Cards or signs with my sayings or advice	Posters or signs with specific theme
High school, college, military or sports memorabilia	Hobby items (e.g., games, crossword puzzles, cribbage board, knitting, etc.)	Maps or travel books showing where I traveled	Memorial candle

5.O. Would you like gifts to be given to attendees of your visitation or reception? If so, what?

_____

_____

_____

_____

_____

_____

_____

Suggestions and examples

Picture of me	Prayer cards or other religious items	Seedlings, seeds, etc. to plant in my memory	Certificates of attendance
Copy of obituary	My favorite thing(s) (e.g., candy, food, drink, movie, TV show, music, game, hobby item, soap, perfume or cologne, etc.)	Shirt, hat, or other item of clothing printed with my name, life details, sayings, etc.	Give away or raffle off my things (e.g., glassware, silverware, tools, clothing, books, artwork, etc.)
Cards with details about my life or anecdotes	Playlist of my favorite songs	Journal, deck of cards, key chain, golf balls / tees, memory stone, etc. printed with my picture, name, initials, life details, sayings, etc.	A book or cards containing my recipes
Cards with my sayings or advice	Locket with my picture		

5.P. Would you like any light or humorous elements incorporated into your visitation or reception? If so, what?

_____

_____

_____

_____

_____

_____

_____

Suggestions and examples			
Have guests recite funny memories about me or my funny sayings	Have fun competitions (e.g., three legged race, wheel barrel race, limbo bar, talent show, Twister, Pictionary, Jenga, etc.)	Encourage everyone to refer to me using a nickname or made up name	Hire an actor to play a funny role (e.g., my lookalike, my long lost lover, spouse or child, someone causing a scene, etc.)
Encourage guests to dress like me (e.g., clothing, hats, shoes, jewelry, makeup, hairstyle, etc.)	Karaoke, humorous group singing, or hire terrible singer	Hire comedian, magician, belly dancer, laughing yoga or meditation instructor, etc.	Pretend spilling of ashes or dropping of casket
Give unique instructions to guests (e.g., walk backward through reception line, speak gibberish, etc.)	Play a funny movie, TV show or comedy album	Hire someone dressed as pirate, zombie, clown, Elvis, Darth Vader, etc.	Pretend voice or noise coming from casket

6 Funeral or Memorial Service

*This is the experience I want
for my family and friends.*

For additional space on any response, use the blank pages in chapter 12 and cross-refer to the relevant question number.

6.A.   Would you like to have a funeral or memorial service? (If no, please skip to chapter 7 of the *Post-Life Instructions Workbook*)

☐   Yes   ☐   No

6.B.   Where would you like the funeral or memorial service held? (Refer to question 5.J. above for suggestions and examples.)

_____

_____

_____

_____

6.C.   When would you like the event held (e.g., what time of day, when in relation to passing, what season, etc.)?

_____

_____

_____

_____

6.D. Do you have specific instructions for your funeral or memorial service? Use the blank pages in chapter 12 for additional space.)

_____
_____
_____
_____
_____
_____
_____
_____
_____
_____
_____
_____
_____
_____
_____
_____
_____
_____

Suggestions on next page

Suggestions and examples			
How long should it last	Theme (e.g., religious, celebration of life, service to others, traditional, roast, etc.)	Dress code (e.g., formal, casual, specific colors, hats or shirts printed with my name / sayings, beachwear, costumes, etc.)	Military funeral or color guard
Specify sequence of events	Religious service or none	Desired arrangement of chairs, seat assignments, design, etc.	Place or pour something on or in grave
Who should officiate (e.g., family, friend, clergy, professional celebrant, etc.)	Specific scriptural or narrative passages, verses, poems or lyrics, and how many readings	Details of any handouts (e.g., content, specific picture, color, etc.)	Release doves, balloons, or lanterns
Assign roles for specific family members or friends (e.g., greeters, ushers, readers, etc.)	Particular music, band or musical instrument	Specific flowers or floral design	Viking funeral or holographic funeral
Committal service	Specific opening or closing	Specific items to have on hand (e.g., coffee, tea, water, wine, champagne, tissues, etc.)	Webcast or recorded by photographer or videographer
Arrange for transportation for: _____			

6.E.   Do you want to be eulogized? If so, who would you like to give your eulogy? (Consider naming backups.)

_____

_____

6.F.   If you want to be eulogized, who should NOT give your eulogy?

_____

_____

6.G.   If you want a eulogy, do you have any specific requests? If you have written your own eulogy, describe where it can be found or confirm you have included a copy with this workbook.

_____

_____

_____

_____

_____

Suggestions and examples			
Instructions for person delivering eulogy (e.g., preferred dress, no crying, tell a joke)	Tone (e.g., serious, loss, lighthearted, upbeat, objective, humorous, sarcastic, etc.)	My traits to avoid discussing (See question 3.H for suggestions)	How eulogy should address my faith, religious beliefs, afterlife, etc.
Single or multiple eulogies	My traits to highlight (See question 3.G. for suggestions)	Other topics to avoid discussing	Anecdote, saying, verse, poem, or lyrics during eulogy or at closing

Continued on next page

Desired length of eulogy	Specific events, accomplishments, or periods of time to highlight	Particular people or relationships not to be mentioned	Funny elements (e.g., eulogizer is late, goes off topic, takes a call, or uses incorrect details)
Theme (e.g., biographical, attributes, life works, etc.)	Particular people or relationships to highlight		

6.H.   Would you like a funeral procession? If so, any specific instructions?

_____

_____

_____

_____

_____

Suggestions and examples

Specific driving route past favorite places or landmarks	Duration of procession and/ or specified stops along the route	Pallbearers role during procession	New Orleans' style jazz funeral procession
Unique instructions (e.g., driving order, drive in reverse, music, throw sticks to block evil spirits)	Incorporate specific vehicles (e.g., my car, sports cars, motorcycles, trucks, police motorcade)	Who should serve as pallbearers	Procession entirely on foot, by horse-drawn carriage, military procession, etc.
Desired size of procession	Decorations or lighting for procession (e.g., signage, strobe lights, etc.)	Special instructions for pallbearers (e.g., what to wear, special routine, etc.)	Funny elements (e.g., stop at drive thru, tie casket or urn to top of car, etc.)

6.I.   Would you like a reception or other event following the funeral or memorial service?

    ▢ Yes   ▢ No

6.J.   If so, please describe timing, location, and other details. (Please refer to chapter 5 for suggestions regarding features of the reception.)

_____

_____

_____

_____

_____

_____

_____

_____

_____

_____

_____

_____

_____

_____

_____

7 Remembrance

Here is how I want you to remember and celebrate me.

For additional space on any response, use the blank pages in chapter 12 and cross-refer to the relevant question number.

7.A.   How would you like to be remembered (e.g., what traits, period of life, acts, etc.)?

_____

_____

_____

7.B.   What about yourself would you prefer that people NOT remember or focus on?

_____

_____

_____

7.C.   Is there a specific way you would prefer that people feel when they think about you after you are gone (e.g., don't feel sad or guilty, think about the good times, don't pity me or judge me, etc.)?

_____

_____

_____

7.D.   Would you like to be memorialized in any specific way?

_____

_____

_____

_____

_____

_____

_____

Suggestions and examples

Solely with the marker or monument described in question 4.D.	Make gifts to specific charity or religious, service, fraternal, or military organization in my name	My nameplate or picture in my favorite place (e.g., place of worship, coffee shop, restaurant, bar, etc.)	Plant a memorial garden, tree or plant
Solely by dealing with my ashes in the manner described in question 4.E.	Dedicate park bench or other items for public use	Create memorial website, Facebook page, etc. or have someone update my social media account (provide password)	Create a book about my life, with my sayings, my recipes, artwork, etc.
Period of mourning, with specific instructions (e.g., wear black, etc.)	Create scholarship or other fund in my name	Create a charm or other jewelry with my name or initials carved on it	Paint a portrait of me or memorialize my face or name in a tattoo, public artwork, etc.
Adopt my pet or a shelter animal			

7.E. Are there any specific ways you would like your family or friends to remember you or mark your passing?

_____

_____

_____

_____

_____

Suggestions and examples			
Think of me when (e.g., birthday, anniversary of my death, holidays, etc.)	Visit my burial site, location where ashes scattered, etc. (and leave flowers or other items)	Set me a place setting at the table (each day, on my birthday, at holiday meals, etc.)	Name a child, pet, car, or other object after me
Honor me by specific acts (e.g., take time for family, act kindly toward others, be creative, finish school, etc.)	Visit my favorite place (e.g., park, coffee shop, restaurant, etc.) or travel to destinations I always wanted to go	Think of different memories of me, look at my pictures, creative works, etc.	Wear my clothes, hat, shoes or perfume or cologne, drive my car, etc.
Volunteer with religious, service, fraternal, or military organization	Hold an event in my memory (e.g., party, cookout, game night, outing, etc.)	Play my favorite movie, TV show, album, game, etc.	Have a memorial drink or smoke, tip a 40, or buy a round of drinks or coffee
Spend time with (or look after) specific person	Post about me on Facebook, Instagram, Twitter, etc.	Include me in your prayers and/or attend religious services	Write me a letter or poem
Follow my sports team	Make my recipe for: _____	Yell my name every time: _____	Spouse remarry or never remarry

8   Other Instructions and Thoughts

These are my wishes for specific people and regarding other unique topics.

For additional space on any response, use the blank pages in chapter 12 and cross-refer to the relevant question number.

8.A.   I designate specific individual(s) to carry out the instructions in this workbook and/or to make decisions on topics not covered herein:

_____

_____

_____

8.B.   What instructions do you have for specific people on your passing?

_____

_____

_____

_____

_____

_____

_____

8.C. What other instructions do you have on your passing?

_____

_____

_____

_____

_____

_____

_____

_____

Suggestions and examples			
Instructions regarding specific personal items not covered by my will	What should happen to my pet	Please apologize for me to: _____	Make sure you: _____
Burn my possessions	Never ready my diary or letters	Return items I borrowed from: _____	Don't ever: _____
Take down my social media accounts (provide passwords in question 11.J.)	Please finish my creative project	Take care of: _____	Deliver flowers, cards, or other gifts on my behalf to my spouse or other person on anniversary, birthday, holidays, at random, etc.
Hold séances to contact my spirit	Spend time with: _____		

9 *Post-Life Instructions Workbook* Summary

If desired, summarize your instructions from the prior chapters and share with others.

Obituary and
Notifications
_____
_____

Body
_____
_____

Visitation or
Reception
_____
_____

Funeral or
Memorial Service
_____
_____

Remembrance
_____
_____

Other Instructions
and Thoughts
_____
_____

10 Signature Page

By signing below, I attest that I have thought about the topics covered in this *Post-Life Instructions Workbook* and desire these instructions to be carried out as my wishes.

While I understand this workbook does not take the place of a will, I would ask any person in possession of these instructions to carry them out to the best of their ability.

Signed: _____

Print Name: _____

Date: _____

If applicable, this *Post-Life Instructions Workbook* replaces my prior instructions dated: _____

Be sure your family and friends know you have completed this *Post-Life Instructions Workbook* **and where it can be found.** For free postcards to infor m others that you have completed this workbook, email postlifeinstructions@gmail.com with your name and mailing address.

11 Additional Information—Personal Administrative Details

Information to aid family and friends in attending to my affairs.

For additional space on any response, use the blank pages in chapter 12 and cross-refer to the relevant question number.

11.A. My social security number:

_____

11.B. Location of my living will, power of attorney, and similar medical instructions:

_____

_____

_____

_____

11.C. Location of my will and name of executor(s):

_____

_____

_____

_____

11.D. Names and contact details of any relevant advisors (e.g., attorney, tax advisor, insurance agent, financial advisor, etc.):

_____

_____

_____

_____

_____

_____

_____

11.E. Details of any insurance or death benefits (e.g., life insurance, accidental death, funeral expense policy, pension death benefits, etc.):

_____

_____

_____

_____

_____

_____

_____

11.F. Bank account details:

Bank Name / Account Number:

_____

Online User ID / Password:

_____

Bank Name / Account Number:

_____

Online User ID / Password:

_____

Bank Name / Account Number:

_____

Online User ID / Password:

_____

(Use the blank pages in chapter 12 for additional space.)

11.G. Other investment information (e.g., collectable pension or governmental benefits, 401(k)/retirement account, stocks, bonds, mutual funds, cryptocurrency, etc.):

_____

_____

_____

_____

_____

(Use the blank pages in chapter 12 for additional space.)

11.H. Other unique assets (e.g., real property, jewelry, art, car, boat, loans made to others, etc.):

_____

_____

_____

_____

_____

11.I. Outstanding debts (e.g., credit card information, mortgage, car or student loans, debts owed to family or friends, outstanding pledge or gift, etc.):

_____

_____

_____

_____

_____

11.J.   My social media accounts to close:

Social media platform:

_____

Username / Password:

_____

Social media platform:

_____

Username / Password:

_____

Social media platform:

_____

Username / Password:

_____

12 Blank Pages

Blank Pages

Made in the USA
Middletown, DE
09 November 2019